I Love Our Earth
Amo nuestra Tierra

Bill Martin Jr. y Michael Sampson
Fotografías de Dan Lipow

i魚i Charlesbridge

For Kelley Fincher—B. M.

For Grete Sampson—M. S.

To my daughter Hannah:
I look forward to sharing and exploring
the whole wonderful world with you—D. L.

Para Kelley Fincher—B. M.

Para Grete Sampson—M. S.

Para mi hija Hannah:
Espero que pueda compartir y explorar
contigo todo nuestro maravilloso mundo—D. L.

Translation copyright 2013 © Charlesbridge; translation by Yanitzia Canetti
Text copyright © 2006 by Bill Martin Jr. and Michael Sampson
Photographs copyright © 2006 by Dan Lipow
All rights reserved, including the right of reproduction in whole or in part in any form. Charlesbridge and colophon are registered
trademarks of Charlesbridge Publishing, Inc.

Published by Charlesbridge
85 Main Street
Watertown, MA 02472
(617) 926-0329
www.charlesbridge.com

LIBRARY OF CONGRESS CATALOGING-IN-PUBLICATION DATA
Martin, Bill, 1916-2004
   [I Love Our Earth Spanish & English]
   I Love Our Earth = Amo nuestra tierra / Bill Martin, Jr., and Michael Sampson ; photographs by
Dan Lipow.
      p. cm.
   ISBN 978-1-58089-556-9 (reinforced for library use)
   ISBN 978-1-58089-557-6 (softcover)
   ISBN 978-1-60734-599-2 (ebook)

1. Earth—Juvenile literature. I. Sampson, Michael R. II. Lipow, Dan, ill. III. Title.
QB631.4.M368 2006
525—dc22   2005006008

Printed in Korea
(hc) 10 9 8 7 6 5 4 3 2 1
(sc) 10 9 8 7 6 5 4 3 2 1

Type set in Ingone, designed by Robert Schenk, Ingrimayne Type
Color separations by Chroma Graphics, Singapore
Printed and bound September 2012 by Sung In Printing in Gunpo-Si, Kyonggi-Do, Korea
Production supervision by Brian G. Walker
Designed by Susan Mallory Sherman and Connie Brown

I love our Earth...
Amo nuestra Tierra...

where green grasses ripple,

donde las hierbas verdes se mecen,

and gray mountains
rise,

*y las montañas
grises se elevan,*

where blue oceans curl,

donde los mares azules se rizan,

and brown deserts swirl.

y los desiertos marrones serpentean.

I love our Earth. . .
Amo nuestra Tierra. . .

for wet forests
that drip,

*por los bosques
húmedos que
gotean,*

and dry winds
that drift,

*y los vientos secos
que ondean,*

for cool mosses
that grow,

*por los frescos
musgos que crecen,*

and warm sunsets
that glow.

*y los atardeceres
cálidos que
resplandecen.*

I love our Earth . . .
Amo nuestra Tierra . . .

when summer stars
flicker,

*cuando brillan las
estrellas del verano,*

and autumn leaves
flame,

*y las hojas del
otoño flamean,*

when winter flakes
blow,

*cuando los copos
del invierno vuelan,*

and spring blossoms
show.

*y florecen los retoños
en la primavera.*

I love our Earth!

¡Amo nuestra Tierra!